Dark Oceans of Divinity

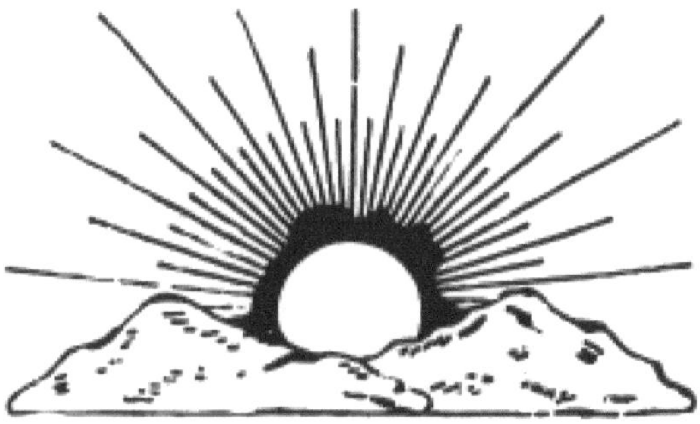

by

Christopher Hivner

ISBN: 978-81-8253-961-7

First Edition: 2022
Rs. 200/-

Cyberwit.net
HIG 45 Kaushambi Kunj, Kalindipuram
Allahabad - 211011 (U.P.) India
http://www.cyberwit.net
Tel: +(91) 9415091004
E-mail: info@cyberwit.net

Contents

Part 1

A Dark Firmament

The Mystery of the Light

Watching the sky,
the black of everything gone
pulsing in the background
while vague light
from another world
circles overhead.
Years and souls
have gone by
and yet the light
still speaks
in a shout about its existence,
a whisper about its origins,
and a cold silence about its past.

The Children of All

A poetic play in 10 Acts

Prologue: The earth is an embattled rock, wobbling on its axis after years of storms, quakes and volcanic eruptions. Humanity is a breath away from extinction; their days spent burying the dead in swamps of diseased water and layers of ash. They have been betrayed. Few venture outside, but there is one man who is willing to fight. He roams the earth railing at the creator, challenging her.

Act I – The Daywalker

I am calling you out,
the woman of the rocks,
entreating you
with passion,
promising you
nothing you need,
threatening all
you hold dear.
Mistress of the mountains
you owe us
and I will
make you pay.

The rain never stops,
doesn't allow us
to breathe,
swallows us

in gloom,
the grayness
of the sky
spreading like cracks
in glass,
trenchant spears
crisscrossing our labors,
piercing the bulbous clouds
to drown us
in pestilence

and you are the cause,
the lady of the earth,
turning verdant land
to blackened ash,
beating hearts
to lifeless slate,
you steal
our world
from us,
the whore of the rivers
watches men die,
lips curling with desire
for the rot
of their bodies.

Come out
to meet me,
bitch of the horizon,
look me in the eyes,
flavor my resolve
with your hatred,
raise the oceans

to fill my lungs
with the brine
of your contempt,
answer my challenge.

Act II – The Goddess of All

I am guilty
of all charges,
I am the bitch,
the whore,
the mistress,
the lady,
the black queen,
the ravager,
the temptress.
I am the ruler
of your estate
and I will suck
the marrow
from your bones

to coat my tongue
with your sorrow.

I will meet you,
daywalker,
on the Sun
or the moon
to devour you.
I will battle

on the ground,
in the water,
or coursing
through the air
and I will
defeat you
with a rage
that melts iron.

You are pitiful,
all of you,
for your anger
toward me,
for following
this lunatic
who threatens me.
I am your
Goddess of All
but do you
worship me?
Do you
beat your breast
pleading for
my attention?
Do you
thank me
for my hardships
providing for you?
Could you do
what I have done,
mortal creatures,
conjuring the magic
to create

a home
for billions?
You abandoned me
and now
I hate you
with the
heat of
a white sun.

I took your earth
because it was
delightful
to see you
in pain.
Desire rises
through the layers
of my
coiled energy,
an orgasm
for the queen.

Act III – The Daywalker

What did you do
for us,
creator of filth?
Our supplications
to your mercy
went unanswered,
crops planted
dead
from drought,

children
with no food,
no guidance
or rules
from our goddess,
killers
walked aside
of farmers,
destroyers
aside of
builders.
You want
worship
then speak
of enjoying
our pain.
We want
nothing more
from you.

Our battlefield
will be none
of the places
you suggest,
demon slut.
I won't spill
your toxic blood
on our land.

We will fight
below ground
in the rot
of death

you have created;
we will do battle,
you and I,
among the corpses
covered in
your tainted stink.

Meet me
and my
army of worms
in the tunnels
of hell
and dance
with our bones
to the song
of your destruction.

Act IV – The Goddess of All

I am
a goddess.
I imagined
your abyss
into being,
so what
makes you think
you can
defeat me?
I am eternal.

Act V – The Daywalker

The battle
has begun
with the
bitch goddess
nowhere in sight.
My worms
do their work,
digging,
corrupting,
breaking our earth
from the inside.
Do you feel
yourself fading,
mighty whore?

Act VI – The Goddess of All

What are you doing?
This isn't a fight;
this is
little pigs
digging in the dirt
for their supper.
Dig,
wee piggies,
dig
your graves.

Interlude: The worms dig tunnels deeper and deeper into the earth's interior, crisscrossing each other, weakening the infrastructure. Soon sinkholes form over the surface of the world, mountains of rock and soil disappearing inside the Earth. The worms dig through that dirt, collapsing it even further. The planet is imploding.

Act VII – The Daywalker

My army
is insatiable,
I could not
stop them
if I tried.
Your world,
queen of feces,
your creation,
is withering.

The tendrils
of hatred
you snap at
your people
find no purchase
now;
we are taking back
our earth,
our world,
our home.
We are returning
to our beginning
in the
soil of life;
we leave you
with nothing.

Act VIII – The Goddess of All

I don't understand
what my piggies
are doing,
destroying your world
faster than
I can.
If I am
to tremble
at your might,
if I am
to bow
at your cleverness,
you will be disappointed.
What do I care
if you
crush yourselves
back to dust?

Act IX – The Daywalker

The mistress of pain,
so full of herself,
lacking in
compassion
and it would seem,
foresight,
prescience,
imagination.
We destroy
our world,
we destroy

ourselves
and take you
with us.

Without
your people,
your humble
progeny,
you have
nothing.
When we
don't exist
neither
do you.

Goodbye
eater of lust,
owner of despair,
without your
creations,
you are
alone,
without our
fear,
you are
empty.
Farewell.

Act X – The Goddess of All

You can't destroy me.

You
    can't
destroy me,
I
    don't need
    you.
Please don't.

Where are
my children?
Their
    heartbeats

    silent.
My beautiful
world
    gone.

From the West

The sun set
in a blazing orange
that stunned even
the priests,
but it did not
dissuade them
from their duties.
The last screams
of the dying sun
turned pale
and darkness
overcame this corner
of the known world.
The priests
flipped their cowls up
to hide the faces
that terrified us,
to start the chant
for awakening the gods,
to become one
with the words
that will seal our fate
in brotherhood
with the wretched gods
who abandoned us
a thousand years ago.
The priests' voices rise,
the chant grows deeper
and we tremble.

Calling on the old ones
to save us
from the marauders
is our last chance,
but it feels like
being surrounded
by evil
while guided by fools.
The ground rumbles,
the stone megalith
protecting the priests
wavers and bends.
Father Asa runs away
screaming,
but the other two
remain stalwart,
chanting in bellows
for the old gods
to be reborn,
protect your creations
from the invaders
of another deity.
The sky splits open,
shards of white light
cut the blackness
like glass,
falling on our monument,
collapsing the stones
onto the priests
whose last words
were of a faith
they no longer
believed in.

As quickly as
the destruction started
it was over.
Blood ran from under
the stones
pooling at our feet,
in the solitude
of a now quiet
starry sky.
We were alone,
no leaders,
no fighters,
and the sound of
marching footsteps
came to our ears
from the west.

Ash and Bone

I am made of flesh,
but my anima
is of a god.
This earth
fails me,
stares through
my incandescence,
tries to corrupt
the true divinity
that lies beneath
my pale skin.
Inferior minds
cannot grasp
what I am,
so they try
to destroy me.
When they took
my eye,
I was imbued
with the strength of Odin,
while I prayed
for peace
and enlightenment,
the mob
tendered my body
with fists
until I felt
the rush
of Buddha's potency

in my soul.
I called
to Allah,
begging for his
spiritual ferocity
while my fellow men
of the flesh
soaked my body
in gasoline
and set me on fire.
I am not of
this world,
I will elevate
to the gates of
heaven,
nirvana,
Valhalla,
the city in the clouds
where the immortals meet
to create
new gods
and I will be accepted,
I must be,
because on this soil
I am only
ash and bone.

The Damned

Fire in the skies
above the night
where black
meets red,
where the gods
play with destiny,
rolling in the clouds
like pale riders,
swathing the first to the last
in the vestments
of the damned.

Fire in the skies
inside the night
where black
scratches red,
where the gods
take their victuals,
hiding in the gardens
like spoiled children,
anointing themselves
with the oils
of privilege.

Fire in the skies
consuming the night
where black
gives way to red,
where the gods

pray to themselves,
wrapped in the shrouds
of burial rites,
begging forgiveness
of the people
they have forsaken.

Gods of Mystic Choice

the intensity of the raven's eyes
burned the forest like oil
dancing in the midnight flames
the feral shrieks of souls echo,
naked and alive I crawl to my savior
but in the cruel shape of fate,
he turns a blind eye

The Night Sky Mortuary

The sky lay over our backs
like an iron sheet,
its dark face
baring fangs
that dripped with the wax
of the melted sun.
The night sky mortuary,
ovens ablaze,
seared our flesh
to brand us as heretics.

We worshipped the Sun,
lived for the light,
prostrated ourselves at the altar
of Mithras,
and the night sky
was enraged.
"Where are my followers?"
he roared,
shaking the mountains
into rubble

and when he
attacked the Sun,
we were lost.
The gloom
encased our flesh
like tar.
We burned,

our mouths moving
in silent pleas
for mercy.

The night sky
has risen,
the overlord
of a charnel house
5000 miles thick,
bodies stacked
to the black

greeting him
with open mouths
and empty eyes.

From his throne
he rules
the dead seas
and scorched land.
"These are my followers,"
he laughs
with menace.
"These are my people."

Preachers of the Feast

Under stripped red skies
wanderers full of grace
look for revelation
in the placement of skulls
left by the invaders.
We chance the daylight,
searching for answers
or death,
an end however fate will allow.

The risk is warranted
say the preachers of the feast,
cowl covered faces in the crowd,
whispering psalms and encomiums
to the Providers.

We pay our alms
and light the candles.
Distinction lost from our lives,
trusting in shadows
and their twisted tongues,
the preachers of the feast
take our faith
and keep it for themselves.

The skies darken
on the eve of the autumnal repast,
bruise-colored clouds
menacing our breaths

while the tables are prepared
and the meat is selected.

My wife and I have survived
one more season
to sit at the Provider's table
and hear the holy men
bless our existence,
but that sentiment
is a vile pronouncement
as our daughter's corpse
is presented
as the main course.

In the Black Forest

The hum,
it razed our flesh
like the edge of a blade,
the horses bucked
desperate to escape,
cold sweat ran
from my mount's fur
as he rose
on his back legs,
kicking at the unseen demons
that filled
the heavy air
with a maddening,
steady wail.

The Violators,
the protectors
of the Black Forest,
surrounded us,
two dozen
desperate men,
seeking a parley
with the Lords of the Void,
begging for
our lives back,
for the sickness
to be lifted
from our families,
for our women

to give birth again,
to eat meat
once more
instead of swallowing
the bitter mist
that falls
from the sky.
We brought
the Lords' wrath
onto ourselves,
now our repentance

forces us
deep into
the Black Forest.

The hum,
it never stops,
as much a warning
to outlanders
not to enter
the forest
as a siren
to the Lords
that they
are not alone.
If we misstep,
the Violators
will eviscerate us
with claws and teeth
that we will
never see
before they plunge

into our bellies
and pull out
our intestines
hooked on the end
of a rotted talon.

I am the leader
of our group
by vote,
not by choice,
a blacksmith
whose hands
are as guilty as any
for bringing our clan
to the rim of hell.

Swords, axes, and spears
pounded out
on my anvil,
heated in my forge,
given to our army
to wield proudly
as they marched
to battle
against the Western Alliance
also known as
the Army of the Void.
But no one had known
they were
the Lords' property.
Why would the Lords
need men
when their magic

strangled us
in our sleep,
ruined our minds,
made us afraid
of the blood
rushing through
our own veins,
when their
feral thoughts
were enough to
bring darkness
to the sun,
why would the Lords
need an army
of men?

They had threatened us,
moving down
from the north
where they had
conquered
a dozen kingdoms,
marching in columns
onto our territory
as though
they owned us,
and we were
but stones
ground into the dirt
under their boots.

We fought back,
the warriors of the

Vestrim valley.
We fought a war
with an enemy
that attacked us
for no reason,
an enemy
that outnumbered us
three to one,
that marched under
a black banner
stained with blood,
and when it
was over,
after the last
wet thud
of steel
into flesh,

we had won the war
and lost everything.

The men of Vestrim
defeated
the invincible
Army of the Void,
celebrated our freedom,
buried our dead,
then watched
as the sickness
spread from
village to village
in a dank fog,
leaving us

barely alive,
broken men
with dying
wives and children,
begging the Lords
to end
their punishment.

The days
went on around us,
but we
couldn't respond;
we became
the gloaming
that had eaten
our world.
The decision was made
by the clan elders
that we must
beg forgiveness
to the Lords of the Void.
The fighters
were left at home,
too weak
to lift a sword,
chosen instead
were farmers,
fishermen, and
tradesmen
to somehow
elicit sympathy
and insist
on our piety.

So here we are now,
petrified
and doubtful,
walking
on the edge
of our destruction.

We dismounted
and left our horses,
the animals
too terrified of
the rasping hum
of the Violators.
We walked along
a narrow path
overgrown with
barbed vines.
The trees
closed in on us
seeming to
grow taller,
the bark
becoming jagged
with teeth,
spiked branches
swiped at us,
tangles of
edged leaves
sliced at our
leather armor.
I heard
several of our men
turn and run,

and I wondered
if we shouldn't all
join them.

The farther in
the trees grew together
so thick
we were
walking single file,
the canopies
keeping out
all but the softest light.
The Violator's hum
had grown steadily
in volume
and was now
overwhelming us,
pressing down
with the weight
of our doom,
our legs
wouldn't raise up.
Grabbing onto
the fiendish trees,
we tried to support
our bodies,
but the Violators
beat us into the ground.

As we lay
on the forest floor
powerless,
we watched

dark green vines
slither over us,
tightening like rope
until we were secured,
prisoners,
sapped of all strength,
driven insane
by the deafening hum
and the
unending darkness.

I waited to die
as this surely
was my fate,
then through the din
and the helplessness
I heard a voice.
It wrapped around
my mind
like soft cloth,
but when it spoke
the words
burned.

"I am the
Lord of Lords,
and I congratulate
your clan
of men
on your victory,
defeating my army."

Before I could stop
I felt myself think

"We're sorry
for our sin against you;
we didn't know
they were your men."

"And if you had?"
The Lord asked.

I hesitated,
then replied,
"We still would have
fought back."

"It is the nature
of man
to fight
when attacked."

"Why attack us though?"
I asked,
trying to understand.

"We subjugate
in many ways.
We are your
overseers,
if you won't
bow to us voluntarily,
we will force you
to your knees
or to your graves."

The Lord's words
were crushing me,

making my life
meaningless,
an endless struggle
that can never
be won,
our victory
in battle,
so hard fought
and important
two seasons ago,
was in vain,
the outcome
sealing a fate
that would have come anyway,
at another time and place.

I struggled
to erase the voice
from my mind,
to put the fire out,
purge my soul
of its restive screams,
finally begging
for it to end.

"Please, my Lord,
haven't you tasted
enough of our flesh?
Save our families,
we are yours
until the end of
this earth."

"A Lord's lusts
cannot be sated,
only dulled.
We considered
your case
before you arrived
and judgment was passed."

"Please, we
can do better."

"Your families
are already dead."

What remained
of my life force
drained out of me
and I could feel
my men
bellowing in anguish
even though
no sound
escaped their throats.

"You and your men
will stay with us
in the Black Forest,
food for our vultures.
Your valley
is now a warning
to others.

We'll see
if all men
are as proud as you were."

The hum
rippled my skin
one last time,
then fell silent
as I felt my body
taking root
in the soil.

A Lamb for Ra

Lying under the fiery sun,
believing I am the chosen one
and all the other poor wretches are bleeding.

Time has embraced me,
you must accept me,
poor, sad dying swans.
    How cruel you must think the sun,
    Ra's holy creation!

When the heat melts the skin from our bones,
    I will survive.
When the rays blind our pleading eyes,
    I will survive.

Pathetic souls who look at me with hatred,
I feel nothing for you.
I deserve to be the Sun God's chosen.
Now I lay here upon the ground,
accepting your blows and curses
because I know
my blood is meant for better things.

The World Over

Along the path
spears of moonlight
alerted us
to the dead
before they transformed.
Our gasoline torches
eulogized their sacrifice
for God or the Devil,
whoever they had preferred.
We didn't ask
which side they had fought for
because we were all one now,
united in surviving
to create our own gods
and start
the world over.

Part 2

In the Shadows of Gehenna

For the Dead

hallowed life taken
friends and loved ones left behind
pain that never ends

freshly dug grave site
the pit that calls forever
rotting for all time

somber day, gray sky
funerals bring rain and worms
feasting on new flesh

time is against us
enemy undefeated
the dead can fight back

soft movement and sounds
the house seems alive at night
can't sleep or think straight

voices penetrate
every hour is misery
won't leave us alone

faces at twilight
in the mirror blanched bone smiles
unrest in our souls

revenge for the dead
spirits among the forest
night remains at large

torment, jealousy
retribution for past sins
we have fallen short

we are for the dead
they have prepared our station
and will meet us there

Illuminating Hell

Clattering hooves
on cobble stone streets
disappear into
night's waiting mouth
leaving silence to reign
over the street of the ripper.
He has laid claim
this night
to one small block
of old London
and one body of flesh
of young Marie,
professional of the trade.

If I were a policeman
or even
a concerned citizen,
perhaps a frightened denizen
or barrister on loan,
I would tell what I've seen
four times before
this new and darkened night.
But I was an artist
in need of a muse
until I stumbled
blindly and drunkenly
into that putrid alley.

I saw things
I could not have described
until then,
images that would not
flee my mind
even after I painted them
over and over again.
Feral strokes
with brushes battered and torn,
colors given to me
by dark gods

to illumine scenes
straight from hell.

I tried,
my God in heaven knows,
I tried to stay away,
to tell the authorities,
to save the pulchritudinous girls
who were my friends,
my confidants,
my solace,
my companions,
to staunch the flow of blood
down my city streets.

Yet, every evening
I watched,
waited for him to go out,
waited for him to choose,
to satiate,
to inspire me.

When he didn't kill,
I didn't create,
drying up inside
like my unused paint.
Evenings passed unrefreshed
and I wondered,
had he given up?
Were the wounded finally safe
and the streets quiet again?

I followed him tonight
in desperation,
convinced at first
he was only out for a walk
but then his pace slowed,
each step deliberate,
and I saw Maria
plying her trade,
invincible and phlegmatic.
She had made
a good night's wages
before my muse
entered her life.
Through a buckling window
I watched in horror,
unable to turn away,
my mind reposited every slash,
every scream, every drop
of precious blood
so that later
when the white heat overcame me
I could commit it to canvas.

My eyes closed
near the end.
Having lain with Maria
only last night,
I recoiled
at each strike against her,
feeling it in my bones,
tasting it in my bile.
My mind swirled
with the painting I hadn't started
yet it was already finished.
Silence had crept in,
evading my brutalized senses.
When I opened my eyes again,
terror tore my throat
like a wolf with a fresh kill.

He was staring at me.
Smiling.
Bloody weapon
like an appendage
drip, drip, dripping onto the floor.
Then he chuckled
from deep in his throat
where words were not allowed.
I was sure I was dead,
the ripper's first male victim.
He left the building,
outside he passed by me
not sparing a glance and said,
"Be sure to remember my good side, painter,"
and the black night
swallowed him up.

He had known about me all along.
My cleverness removed,
I found I could not paint.
His final killing
remains a lost masterpiece,
my mind as blank
as raw slate.
I told the authorities all I knew,
months after,
by then, too late.
Now I sit in a cell
for withholding knowledge
while the ripper roams free.
A laugh bellows outside
in the distance,
and my bowels tighten.

Wishing Well

If the sisters could talk,
would they talk about me?
Can they see me
in their dreams
as the mother can?
Could they feel her screams
while in the womb?

If the sisters could talk,
would they talk about me
and the pain the world is in,
the pain I have caused,
the pain of knowing,
and having no choice?

The doubt.
That's what pleases me,
the doubt the mother feels
about her involvement.
"I didn't, I couldn't"
she weeps into the carpet
on the floor
again.
Sweet Lorraine and a bottle of wine.

If the girls could love,
would they love me?
But they can't love
or regret

or go to the prom
or watch the fires burn
or tell Mommy

because Mommy already knows,
and it's all so pale.
She won't fight back
to save their tiny
souls.
Sweet Lorraine and a bottle.

If the girls could choose,
would they pick me
as Daddy?
Throw a penny down the wishing well
and open the gates of hell.
Throw a penny down the wishing well,
I'll never tell.

Until the Dawn

In the flames,
over the dunes,
beyond the resting stars,
they will pursue you.
Until the dawn
pushes you through
the boundless door
they will sharpen
Talwar blades
in the wind of battle.
They can read the sand
for where you've been,
administer the opiates
for where you'll go,
and summon the ancient gods
to discern where you are.
    Until the dawn
    washes you ashore
    from a midnight baggala,
    they will stand
knee deep in corpses
to find you.
The desert allure
brought you to this place
of destruction,
brought you to
their second sight,
left you for consumption
with no psalms

for your righteous soul.
    Until the dawn
    allows you
    to escape,
    the guards of Persia
    will call your song
to the savage night.

In the Teeth

We hide
among the wisps of smoke,
an evanescent message
to an underworld
in the teeth,
faceless to the living,
but the dead
know our names,
the dead
walk a straight line,
dragging skulls behind them
as a warning.

We hide
in the drifts of sand,
under the choking water,
behind the hem of Mother's dress,
waiting for the new moon
to offer shelter
and Mars
to profane us,
before
the dead
sound their Klaxon
that we've been found.

We hide
so we don't have to face
the evening silk.

The abyss tempts
in slow, loving
kisses
and words
spoken
with a liquid tongue.
The seduction
covers the clatter
of skulls.
The dead
are here.

We hid
for as long
as we could
under the downy feathers
of protective wings.
We told
our stories
to the passing light,
leaving our words
in the dirt
and on the rocks
to be heard
one day
by a future generation,
listening for screams
on the wind.

We hid
and we died,
leaving the fight
to others,

our ancient bones
dust in the
smoke-and-ash choked sky
of Armageddon.

Internal Death

Into the abyss
I fall from my throne.
Raked by claws,
flesh torn by razor teeth,
the reapers
bleed me
to the desert of maggots.
I made a pact
with the wrong faction,
my grab for the winter ice
has been deflected
by unseen hands
covered with the oil
of internal death.
I will never land
on solid ground,
the talons that stab me
will never retract.
This is my eternal castle,
a black tunnel
straight down.

Neverworld

First
there was spirit
with the wings of broken angels,
spoiling the Overworld
in a reign
of darkness stolen from light,
hatred cut out of love with a blunt blade,
vengeance burned from forgiveness using a gasoline flame.

Next
there were corporeal remnants,
scurrying like disease
from one corpse to another,
the wasted leftovers in the new Fuckedworld,
palming any strip of uninfected flesh
to eat later
when the Sun left them
and the only living was to hide
among the bones.

Last
there was the King,
black beard thick with segmented worms
burrowing for the virus that will end their torment
as the single living creatures of Neverworld,
a hollow space
resplendent in the echoes of choking screams
and acrid wind blowing the dry husks
of human faces
over the landscape like tumbleweed.

Dance, Marionette, Dance

no wind
no mountains
no grass
no trees
no clouds
no smoke
no birds
no Sun
no stars
no family
no friends
no jokes
no music
no sound at all

heat from nowhere
and everywhere
seething
pulsing
your body engorged
with radiation
darkness
dripping like oil
sealing to blistered skin
black sand
underfoot
a beach of nothing

and you walk

until

you try to collapse
but hands
from behind the curtain
lift you back up
and push you on

and you walk

until

spinning in a circle
looking for something
looking for light
searching for nature
yearning for a companion
or a whisper
or a shape
a drop of rain
something to drown out the silence
to wash away
the pitch black
give you a direction
spinning in a circle
no relief from the heat
turning your organs to jelly
. . . from the heat . . .
the heat
eyeballs melting like wax to your sockets
the heat . . .

and you collapse into the sand
only to be yanked to your feet
muscles cramping
turning to stone under your skin
you hear nothing
see only blackness
but you know what to do

and you walk

Maroon-Black (Salvation's End)

Telluric rumbles
signal the end,
a tocsin blared through
the bleeding ears
of those who are left,
but we're on our knees,
bleating raw-throated pleas
to the wrong gods,
crying tears
that we had saved up,
a special reserve
for courting salvation.

Monster's engine
firing red
on all cylinders,
a beast of heat and filth
spewing guttural words
that cut as the truth
in all languages and dialects,
vestigial fires from
the mile-wide mouth
lick the sky
to ignite Earth's gasses
so we burn
as another sun.

The earth splits open,
the inchoate creature

demanding attention,
throwing mountains
through the atmosphere,
strata quakes
as the eyes open
for the first time,
maroon-black
and swimming in
ten-thousand-year-old corpses.

Transformed from the inside,
the Earth has become
the guts of the beast,
so why do we stand
and stare
instead of run,
why are some
leaping into the maw,
smiling as though free?

I can see the end
but refuse to embrace it,
I can see through the fire
to another world.

When the Shadows

When the shadows drop
and they always drop,
my infected being crawls out
from its daylight grave of steam.
When the shadows cover
and they always cover,
I can walk the holy ground
unafraid.
When the shadows descend
and they always descend,
my dead lover rises from
her sepulcher
and takes my hand.
When the shadows caress my skin
with a velveteen tongue,
we embrace
under a spear of moonlight.
When the shadows beckon
and they always beckon,
we make love so passionate
the wind ignites a spark.
When the shadows fall
and they always fall,
we sanctify the union
of our decrepit, bloodless hearts,
her softly rotting lips
brush my own
and we are one,
we are whole.

When the shadows disturb the day
as they always will,
my lover
dances over graves,
whispers into the souls of mortal men,
sings with the dulcet thickness of death in her throat,
and I revel in her spirit.
When the shadows creep over the land,
spreading like liquid,
we stand in awe of the darkness's grace.
As the black seeps into the pores of our bones,
we embrace a final time.
When the shadows lift
and they always lift,
my lover says goodbye.
As she fades to a misty outline,
returning to her resting place,
the night is gone
and a new day risen,
a day that will bring the shadows.

My Wretched Soul

She danced,
from the white days
to the black nights,
from the dull days
to the dangerous nights
she danced.

She called my name
in smoke
from her serpent tongue.
She fed me
from her hips,
soothed me with her stare.
She bought me
for nothing
and sold my remains
for rubies and sapphires.

Lift the veil
and the jinn fades,
back into darkness,
leaving me in the light,
suckling to her breast,
facing my rescuers
and wishing them dead.

She dances
for me
and my wretched soul.

A Nod and a Sigh

Prometheus brought the fire
as a gift,
but we let it burn
out of control,
and it raged until
the rivers dried to
beds of silt and ash.
The oceans boiled away,
leaving a graveyard of bones.
Now we walk the Earth
in search of water
to quench our thirst,
slake our desire for survival.

Crossing the Atlantic,
remains of elegant sea creatures
rattling under our feet,
sleeping on layers of brittle kelp,
burning marrow to stay warm,
we meet others seeking the same as us.
We bond over stories
of ancient gods and titans,
memories of swimming
in the diamond blue water;
we bond over
not wanting it to end
with a nod and a sigh.

We soon realize the truth:
there will be no interference from the supernatural,
no assistance from other realms,
and not a drop of water to drink.
We press away our dreams,
spend our remaining currency
in a last game of cards,
a pair of natural sevens
takes the last pot,
so we sit on the bones
of all who went before us,
grasping tightly onto
the suicide king,
and wait.

Down There

Down there,
through the fog
and the trees.
That's where it came from.
You can still hear screams.
Down there,
that's where it dragged a body
over the hill,
where the moon doesn't shine.
There's a trail to follow.
The screams still echo
from down there.
I can smell freshly turned dirt,
copper coats my tongue.
I am only dimly aware of my voice wailing
as the beast emerges,
talons from the mist
that pull me down
to waiting fires,
and I finally realize
the screams were always mine.

No Clothes for the King

Ring around the rosie,
pocketful of matches
ashes, ashes
we'll burn it all to the ground

Ring around the rosie,
pocketful of dead things
ashes, ashes
no one gets out alive

Ring around the rosie,
pocketful of quiet
ashes, ashes
the sound of annihilation

Part 3

Light for Darkness

If I

If I fall asleep,
don't let the night devour me.
If I cry for my mother,
protect my face so God will recognize me.
If I bleed,
bleed with me.
If I lose consciousness,
save my body from the feeders.
If you love me,
don't let me go easily.
If I wake the next morning,
bathe me in perfume and oils
to prepare for the
coming dusk.

Fertile Soil

The mist surrounds me
forming to my skin,
a shift
to hide me
from the angelic voices
that fill
this ancient forest,
soughing through
the tree limbs,
incantations of bloodlust
from God's avengers.
They search for me,
a syphilitic demon
guilty of spreading
madness
among the believers,
guilty of laughter
as the visions
chewed on their brains
like carnivorous insects.
My master has created
an organic shroud
so I may walk
between my destroyers
untouched
by the vengeance
they seek.
I complete the camouflage
by changing my shape

from lizard-like body
with raking claws
to a proud,
majestic oak tree,
my woody flesh
blending with the other inhabitants
of the forest.

Now that I am safe,
I can relax
and relish my memories
of the humans
I have wronged,
all the words
I whispered in their ears,
the false ideas
that sprang forth
and the passions
with which they chased
their vile dreams.
All I had to do
was suggest,
one small flower
planted in the
fertile soil of
their own imaginations,
and their true hearts emerged,
far worse than mine.
My own personal darkness
doesn't plunge
to human depths,
but I receive the blame.
I am the one

who is hunted
by God and his mercenaries.

The air is quiet,
my surroundings still,
the mist is burning off,
and from my lofty place
I can see
the countryside awaken.
Another new day
for me to ply my trade
on the lumps of flesh
and their emotional
candy centers.
I stretch my limbs,
sprinkling the ground
with leaves.
When I open my eyes,
I realize
something is wrong.
I am being watched,
unseen eyes
stroking me with anger.
Bright sunlight
forms a halo
around my fellow oaks,
their shapes changing
until before me
stand six Angels,
wings blazing with fire,
each with
an axe
in its hands.

The Dark Sky

The light leads me
into the desert,
no horse or camel,
no shoes on my feet.
The night makes the sand cool
beneath my skin
and the breeze,
a hand cupping my face.
I see a tent ahead
but no life.
The flaps blow in the wind,
no breath joins it,
no voices dissolve into
the dark sky.
I enter the tent
to the smell of incense
still burning,
and of burnt meat
left behind,
the sweetness of fresh fruit
hangs like perfume
in the air.
My bare feet
walk on thick rugs
overlapping each other.
I place a strip of lamb
in my mouth,
the succulent juice
wetting my lips.

I find wine and drink heartily,
refilling my glass
more than once.
I would like to lie down
and sleep,
but they are already too far ahead of me,
so I grab a half dozen dates
and exit the tent.
Back into the night air,
the food a balm
for my desperation
but not the Godsend
of finding
the djinn
who stole my essence,
the ether that
makes me human.
He travels as a nomad of means,
using my life force
to gather others,
to steal what he can't possess
on this plane.
He is all smoke
and black ministrations,
suffusing flesh and bone
into spirit and dreams.
He is an evil loosed
from the dark sky
by ancient lightning
who found me
at my weakest
and turned me to dust,
a shell of loose skin

and empty veins,
bloodless, lifeless, dull, and morose.
If not for the guiding light
of the moon,
I could never follow,
but I am losing my beacon
as the days press on,
and the black djinn
remains ahead of me,
surrounding at all times
with his expanse overhead,
reminding me of his power,
his breadth and reach
sagging my will,
but I want back
what is mine,
so I walk on,
sucking in the sloppy juice
of the dates.
My light leads me forward,
one step before the other,
walking in the footprints
left behind
by my enemy,
sensing my anima
on the air,
taking it in,
swallowing it in gulps
to fill my empty balloon of a body.
"You have stolen ME!"
I scream at the dark sky,
and I feel it slap my face
with a rumble

and flash of lightning.
I drop to my knees,
tearing my throat out,
"Where do I begin and end?"
The blackness rolls
like ocean waves
over the moon
and I am trapped
without light,
surrounded, penetrated
by the contaminated djinn.
"Where am I?"
I roar,
feeling a cold arm
reach down my throat
and fill me with darkness.
My body bloated,
skin pulled taut,
eyeballs ready to burst.
I feel my bowels drop,
my groin shrivel,
my legs bandy,
and then just as violently
as he has violated me,
the malevolent djinn
leaves my body,
expanding back into the deep, dark sky.
"You have me," I whisper
before collapsing to the dunes,
my mouth filling with sand.
"But you will never conquer me."

Deathscream

One angel's
broken body
found in the water
started the war.

God grieved at
seeing his guardian dead,
taking the time to weep
before showing his anger.

God opened up heaven,
the supernatural light
shining down to lash the world
with frenetic energy.

With the word spoken,
Gabriel's trumpet blew
and every man, woman, and child
trembled.

The angels of the Lord
swept through the sky,
fire trailing from
pure white wings,

searching every
spade full of dirt
and every breath of oxygen
for God's enemies.

They found the demons
walking the earth
in their skin suits,
eyes gleaming with hatred.

The fury of the Father
erupted from the
angel's throats
in a howling deathscream

while the gates of hell
were overrun
with Satan's parasites,
sent to join in the fight,

giving them the advantage,
the Devil sending
wave after wave
of virulent creatures.

Darkness consumed
the Earth
when evil
outnumbered good.

Spires of acrid smoke
stretched into the sky
like gnarled fingers
reaching for God,

and he responded
with a sweep
of his hand,
moving the Sun closer.

The heat engulfed the planet
in flames,
boiling the oceans,
scorching every living thing

but there was no time
for pain
as it happened
in the blink of an eye.

Nothing escaped
the wrath of God,
not angel nor demon
nor human,

and then there was calm.
The last embers still glowed
as the angels unfurled
their protective wings,

rising back to heaven
black ash streaming from their swords,
carrying the body
of their fallen friend.

A searing wind blew
like a sandstorm
over the land,
collecting the husks

of the wasted demons,
depositing them in the portals
back to the underworld,
a gift for the Deceiver.

The unharmed innocents
emerged to a blackened landscape,
reciting prayers
and beginning to rebuild.

God named each one,
guiding their steps,
studying their movements,
watching for signs

of another infestation
from below,
another craven attempt
to take what's rightfully His.

Angels line the path to heaven,
ever vigilant
for God's command
to reap vengeance.

Daniel

I would have put
flowers
on his grave,
but I knew
he would be pissed.
Adornments on the headstone
meant he was dead
and people cared.
He was only
sort of dead,
and he hated
anyone giving a shit
that he was gone.

I visited once
a week anyway,
he knew
damn well I would.
We didn't have
deep conversations,
didn't "share"
a beer,
mostly I stared
at the ground
and cursed him
for being
my half-brother
and for being
a demon.

Every time I think
of the word
I can feel Daniel
punch me
from the inside.
He's not a demon
by choice,
that would be
his father's fault.
My dad sold insurance,
Daniel's
reaped souls,
the man himself,
Satan, in all
his ruby skinned glory.

How did
our mom
get involved with
the man downstairs?
First of all,
he went by
Andy back then.
Andrew Teufel from
New Freedom, PA.
Yes, Andy loved
his irony,
and his tequila and lime,
which so did
our mom, unfortunately.
My father was gone,
left town with
a carton of cigarettes,

$300 cash
and the 17-year-old
clerk at the mini mart.
Mom was numb.
Andy had
a slippery tongue,
bottomless pockets
and looked like a
slightly inebriated Kevin Bacon.

Why Old Scratch wanted to
get with my mom
is understandable,
and disturbing,
but why he wanted to
get married
is a mystery.
Nevertheless, at age five
I had a stepdad
who would leave Mom
passed out across the bed
and stay out
until morning.
I waited up for him once,
he stumbled in
the back door,
his face crimson
and sweating,
horns still protruding
from his
balding forehead.
His hands were shaking
and I thought

I saw blood,
but what did I know,
and who
was I going to tell?
I was five
and stepdaddy
had knobs
and red skin.

A day after
my seventh birthday,
which we celebrated
in the emergency room
with a half-inflated balloon
and desperate promises
to "make it up" to me,
I had a brother.
He was early,
and big,
and had a tail
which the doctor
quietly snipped off
much to stepdaddy's anger.
Punches were thrown,
Andy got arrested,
he smiled wickedly
in my direction
as they dragged him
down the hallway.
I looked at Mom
holding my brother
and I'd never seen
such sadness.

Mom used to go to church,
we kept a Bible
on an end table
by the television,
I never opened it,
never saw her
crack it either,
but she gathered comfort
in it being there
and in telling people
she believed.
Every possible baby name
she picked out
was from the Bible.
Andy was not happy.
He told us
many times,
while spitting
bourbon flavored saliva,
that, oh yes,
he believed,
but he hated God
with all of
his passion.
Mom said
"I don't care,
our son's name is Daniel."
And that was that.
The one
and only time
she stood up
to the red fleshed bastard
was to name

her child.
I stood behind her
when she made
her proclamation,
ready to fight for her
with all of my
puny-child strength,
but the battle
was never waged.
Andy looked stupidly
from his wife
to me,
shook his
cock-eyed head
and left the house.

Stepdaddy ignored me
all day,
every day.
Daniel was his
only concern,
but the boy didn't turn out
like he expected.
My brother and I
got close
despite Andy's attempts
to keep us apart.
Daniel didn't like
being separated
from me,
stuck up for me,
told his father off
for my benefit.

Andy's thick hands
started to find
my kidneys
on a daily basis.
Daniel was so
young he
couldn't have understood,
but he wasn't normal
in so many ways.

Andy wanted
to train his son.
Daniel ignored him
until the beatings
stopped and only
then would he listen,
although behind
Andy's back,
the little shit
would wink at me.
What the hell
was going on?
I used to lie
on my bed
staring at the ceiling,
asking a God
I wasn't sure was there,
if his nemesis,
Lucifer, was really
downstairs in our basement
teaching life lessons
to my baby brother,
an actual,

100% guaranteed,
real McCoy
spawn of Satan.

Our mom
didn't get to
spend much time
with Daniel.
When she tried,
Andy would intervene
and Danny
would go with him
to keep the
drunk fuck's hands
off of us.
Our best times
were when Andy
went out at night
and Daniel
was still too young
to go along.
The two of us
would crawl into
Mom's bed,
curl up next to her
and watch
reruns of the
Dick van Dyke Show,
her favorite,
and fall asleep
to the sound
of Mother's laughter.

We were seven
years apart,
but Daniel was
my best friend,
and it pissed Andy off.
He wanted
to bloody me,
but now I was old enough
to fight back,
not that I could do
any damage,
yet Andy
grew frustrated that
I wasn't afraid
of him anymore.
Danny, on the other hand,
had grown
weirdly powerful,
more so every day,
and I think
Andy actually got scared.
If he was
who I thought he was,
then stepdaddy
should be in control,
but he wavered,
sometimes ruling,
other times
unsure of himself,
staring hard
at Daniel with eyes
that burned
like a bonfire

and a mouth
that muttered vulgarities
under his breath.

When I was 18,
I moved out.
Daniel convinced Mom
to come with me.
She didn't want to leave him,
only 11 years old,
but he was
different,
and deep down
she knew
there was little of her
inside of Daniel.
But he knew who,
and what, she was
to him;
he called her Mother

until the day
she died.

The house was
a circus,
and Andy was the
evil clown,
lurching and listing
from room to room,
drowning in
Boone's Farm,
bellowing instructions

for Danny
in his infernal tongue,
proclaiming himself
master of earth
and air,
water and fire,
the overseer of
all life and
the king
of death.
Daniel listened
to none of it.

Andy retreated
to the cellar,
locking himself in,
roaring in
a language even
Daniel couldn't understand.
The house shook,
windows imploded,
overwhelming heat
permeated the walls,
turning the building
into a two-story
Cape Cod oven.
For the first time
Daniel was confused,
he didn't know
what Andy's behavior
meant or
what to do,
so he left

his father alone,
stayed with me and Mom
for a while,
and every time
he checked
on Andy,
stepdaddy was still
in the cellar.
The speaking in gibberish
had stopped
but the heat
remained.
I tried to walk in
with Danny once,
my skin blistered,
internal organs
felt loose
and watery
before my brother
shoved me
back outside.

Things changed.
Daniel lost his
sense of humor,
stopped calling,
left Mom and me
to ourselves.
If I tried
to see him,
he got angry,
then left a gift
on the stoop

to apologize.
I did my best
Dick Tracy once
and watched
from an
abandoned house
across the street.
Andy was
out of the cellar
and lucid.
He had stopped drinking,
cleaned up
and grown stronger,
his skin was back
to deep crimson,
his horns
were out
to stay,
no matter who saw,
and they were thick,
sharp, and menacing.
The look
in his eyes was a
pure black void.
Andy Teufel
was gone.

He looked directly
at me
that day
even though
I was behind a wall
peering through a hole

in the concrete.
He knew
I was there.
When darkness fell,
Daniel emerged
from the house,
looking gaunt
and reluctant,
letting Andy
steer him
down the street.
I thought about
following them
but stepdaddy turned
around sharply,
staring through the concrete,
through my skin,
into my body.
My chest constricted,
throat closed,
couldn't breathe
until I passed out.
I came to
with a burn
on my chest
around my heart
and stale air
wheezing from my lungs.

I went off
to college,
Daniel and I
rarely spoke anymore.

I got
an occasional call
at 3 a.m.,
asking if I was studying
or drinking,
how many
college girls
had I collected,
instructed me to
keep my head down,
stay out
of trouble.
He always sounded
flat, like
a weight was tied
around his tongue,
and hesitant
as if he wanted
to say more,
do more,
be my brother again.
Then he
would spill out an
"I love you"
and be gone.

Stories spread
across town
about
the man
with "fire eyes"
who would
eat your soul

and leave
nothing behind except
an oily puddle
and "the teacher"
who hid in
the shadows
waiting to feed
from his pupil's
leathery hand.
The drug dens
cleared out,
alleys were vacated,
everyone started
living in the light,

but no one could
stop Andy,
he found his victims
with ease
and Daniel
was the dutiful son,
playing Daddy's game
to keep peace
for us and
for himself.
Whatever Andy
had done
in the basement
of our old house,
he had transformed
and he was
the ne plus ultra
of Shit Town.

Mom died.
The bitterness
and despair
left her a husk,
the alcohol
drowned her veins,
the sorrow
painted her body
pale.
I was selling
what I could
to give her
a nice funeral
when $6000
appeared in the mailbox,
the edges of the bills
singed from the heat
of Daniel's hands.
I didn't think
he would
show up to
the burial,
but I felt
a hot spot on
the back of my neck,
turned
and saw a
hulking shadow
behind the mausoleums,
a shade that
put a hand
over its heart
and bowed its head.

Daniel had always
shed tears freely
for Mom,
never embarrassed,
never wavered
in his devotion,
no matter
what payment
Andy rendered.
Daniel had become
a slave
to his
demon progenitor
but stepdaddy couldn't
force him
to give up
his family.

I hadn't been
face to face
with my brother
in years,
our contact was
late night phone calls
or an otherworldly feeling
I was
being watched.
On his 18th birthday,
Daniel appeared
at my back door.

My God
he was a behemoth,

filled the doorway
and then some,
though he tried
to hide
under a flowing
black duster.
"I need to see you,"
he told me,
my fingers hovering
over the light switch.
He didn't balk,
so I flicked
and a weak
40 watt beam
shone on
scarred skin
stretched over bone
that looked like
it had been
chiseled from the side
of a mountain.
His hair
was shaggy and unkempt,
covering his entire head,
but it couldn't hide
the horns,
stubby points
of thick bone
jutting out at me
like a threat.

I got drunk
on a half case

of beer
while Daniel
poured it down
his throat
unaffected,
we laughed together
for the first time
since we were kids,
sitting on the dirty
kitchen floor
like we were
getting away
with something.
I told my
baby brother
all the college stories
I never could,
every party,
every girlfriend,
every prank
and drunken night
I could remember.

At the sight of 4 a.m.,
after a long silence,
I asked Daniel
why he had come.
He smiled
and then said,
in a voice that
chewed glass
and spit out blood,
that he was

near the end.
Another silence
left me obliged
to ask
"The end of what?"
He slumped
against the wall,
bounced a beer can
off of my head
with a chuckle
and said,
"Eternity."

I remember
staring into his eyes
at the flames
that danced
in rhythm
with nothing.
His answer made no sense
but I understood.
He took my hand
and held it,
the tears
that Andy had tried
to destroy
flowed without remorse.
I secretly hoped
that stepdaddy
was somewhere filthy,
covered in piss,
raging to
a congregation

of rats
about his son's
betrayal.

I heard Daniel say
"Love you"
before I passed out,
and when I woke
the next day,
I found his ring
pushed awkwardly
onto my pinkie.
I pulled it off,
rolling the faded, scratched
green plastic
around in my palm.
Froot Loops,
that was the cereal
it came out of.
I pulled mine
off my key ring.
With my thumbnail
I flipped open
the secret compartments.
Inside of each was
a scrap of paper,
folded into a tight ball.
I flattened both out,
held them up
to the light,
matching the
jagged edge together
like puzzle pieces.

A picture of
two brothers,
ages 5 and 12,
arms around shoulders,
rabbit ears
behind each other's heads.

The city exploded.
Fires burned
out of control,
bodies floated
to shore,
spit up by the river,
people stormed
police stations
begging for them
to do something,
but the police
didn't know
what the hell
was going on.
The Sun never seemed
to shine anymore,
but how was that
even possible?
It was October
and it was
a thousand degrees
outside.

The Devil
was here,
on earth,

stalking the city,
that's what the
street people said,
El Diablo, El Jefe,
the Night Demon,
Master of the Darkness,
the Black Soul Eater.

I saw things
I wasn't supposed to
the night
my house
burned down.
Asleep on the couch
I never heard
Andy come in,
he woke me,
pummeling my kidneys
for old time's sake.
I was on my knees
puking blood
when he rubbed
two fingers together
like tinder sticks,
producing a
bright orange
orb of flames
which he threw
against the wall,
and it exploded
like 4th of July.
Only after
the burning started,

did I smell
the gasoline.

My legs were
begging to run,
but there was
nowhere to go,
and then
my body
was in the air,
thrown over
someone's shoulders,
a fireman
I assumed,
until we got outside
and Daniel
sat me on a stoop
across the street.

Before I could
say thank you,
he was pelted
with fireballs
from behind,
his body erupting
in hissing, snapping,
snake-like flames.

And he winked at me.

Daniel turned around,
staring at his father
who stood

in the middle
of the street
in full
Satanic regalia:
cloven hooves,
black, curved horns,
red skin
giving off
so much heat
the asphalt
below his feet
cracked and bubbled.
Andy's eyes
were obsidian,
dead.

Daniel shook off
his duster;
he was mountainous,
Andy's abomination
set loose
on Earth
to wreak havoc
and collect
the useless souls
that could be
traded for
a drink,
a smoke,
or a fuck.

The time had come
for a showdown,

and I knew
how the fight
would end.
Daniel did his best
to never be
what Andy wanted
him to be,
but his powers
were limited
even if
his recalcitrance
was boundless.
I cowered
in a doorway
while my brother
fought
the Devil.

Daniel's muscles
rippled like the
waves on the ocean
as energy
built up under
his skin,
and he changed colors,
from white
to pink to red
to auburn
to black.
His body like
a piece
of overripe fruit,
his skin peeled,

falling to the ground
with a
liquid plop.

Pure fire,
controlled flames,
a fulminating
furnace of rage,
Daniel had transformed.

He opened
his mouth
and roared.

The ground rumbled,
car alarms blared,
children screamed,
men pissed themselves.

Daniel leaned
his head back
to howl at the sky,
and he sucked
the stars
down his throat.
The darkness
constricted
the flesh of the world.

Phantasms and delusions
devoured
our minds,
wraiths and demons

sang canticles
of destruction
into our pink flesh.
I tried to
call out
to Daniel
but the pressure

created a stillness

where the universe stopped

completely

and I saw
my brother
glowing.

Daniel's body
exploded
sending brilliant, blinding,
effervescent,
white hot
light
into the world.
The darkness
fractured,
falling to the ground
in pieces,
sharp and distinct.
The stars
reappeared,
hanging in
the atmosphere

of rebirth
like pearls
from my mother's neck.

I shielded my eyes,
biting into
my arm
to stay sane.
I heard crackling,
spitting,
humming,
and dared a look.
Photons sparked
and jumped
in the place where
Daniel had stood,
jittery balls
of luminescence
that fused
together
one after another,
climbing higher,
curving into the pattern
of my baby brother.

Daniel shimmered
as he stood
in the road,
appearing as he did
when we were young,
a boy of ten
or eleven,
his being

a silvery shadow,
arms raised
in supplication.
I dared to
open my eyes,
finding the light
warm and inviting,
soothing my vision,
creating a softness
that bedded
me down
and held me
in relief.

Daniel's face
was beatific,
his eyes glimmered
like sunlight
on the surface
of the water.
His body
was swimming
with rays of light
that snaked
through him,
forming pathways
that radiated
peace and beneficence,

and then he was gone.

I blinked.

Blinked again,
a line of blood
left my eye,
rolling down
my cheek.
I felt it
slide over
my lip
and down my chin.

There was a crater
where Daniel
had stood.
A blackened,
smoking,
festering,
aphotic hole.

At the edges
there were
embers,
tiny, glowing,
orange and red
stipples
that spit
and crackled,
meandering in
a haphazard
trail to follow,
a path,
narrow and formless,
that led
to Satan's
upturned palm.

Andy Teufel,
the Devil
disguised as
middle management,
stood silently,
sans emotion,
staring at
the emptiness
he had created.
He walked to
the spot,
his hooves
clacking on the macadam,
echoing in the
stillness,
thudding off
the brick and mortar
of the buildings.

The profane prince
threw one
last sneer
in my direction
before jumping
into the hole.

Then it closed.

Daniel's reign
had ended.

I bought
the cemetery plot

because I
needed to remember
my brother,
the one who
ate crayons,
peed his bed,
hated cauliflower
even more than me.
He was real,
flesh and blood,
tears and
dirty jokes.

I wiped
some mud
off the face
of the tombstone:
Daniel,
loving son
and brother,
then placed
a single lily
on the ground.
It took only
a second
before I felt
the punch in my gut.

I smiled
and walked away.

Acknowledgments

The following poems were previously published elsewhere. Edited and updated versions appear in this collection.

The Mystery of the Light was originally published in *The Catbird Seat* 1999

Gods of Mystic Choice was originally published in *the kore* 1994

Preachers of the Feast was originally published in *Deadman's Tome* 2010

A Lamb for Ra was originally published in *Cemetery Moon* 2007

The World Over was originally published in *Dark Gothic Resurrected* 2011

For the Dead was originally published in the *Screaming Poets Anthology* in 2012

Illuminating Hell was originally published in *Niteblade* 2009

Wishing Well was originally published in *The Horror Zine* 2010

In the Teeth was originally published in *Moonlight Glinting from the Blade* in 2011

Neverworld was originally published in the *Screaming Poets Anthology* in 2012

Dance, Marionette, Dance was originally published in *Nightshopping Netzine* 2003

When the Shadows was originally published in *Edgar* in 1999

A Nod and a Sigh was originally published in the *Screaming Poets Anthology* in 2012

Internal Death was originally published in *The Horror Zine* 2017

Down There was originally published in *Dark Moon Rising* 2002

If I was originally published in *Siren's Call Ezine* 2021

Fertile Soil was originally published in *Fantastic Horror* 2013

www.ingramcontent.com/pod-product-compliance
Lightning Source LLC
Chambersburg PA
CBHW050019170726
48282CB00025B/469